Today Is Monday in Kentucky

Copyright © 2012, 2022 by Johnette Downing

Illustrations © 2012, 2022 by Deborah Ousley Kadair

All rights reserved

Published by
Wiggle Worm Publishing
PO Box 13367
New Orleans, LA 70185

For Virginia Carter, Kathleen Pool, and Rick Gruber, whose love of and knowledge about Kentucky's cuisine and culture made this book possible. A special thanks to Alan Rapp and Kern's Kitchen, Inc. — JD

To my nieces Meagan and Emily. You are my special girls! Love you. — DOK

Today Is Monday in Kentucky

Traditional Song Adapted by Johnette Downing

Illustrated by Deborah Ousley Kadair

Wiggle Worm Publishing

New Orleans 2022

Today Is Monday.

Today is Monday.
Monday **burgoo**.

All you lucky children
come and eat it up.
Come and eat it up!

Today Is Tuesday.

Today is Tuesday.
Tuesday **sorghum**,
Monday burgoo.

All you lucky children
come and eat it up.
Come and eat it up!

Today Is Wednesday.

Today is Wednesday.
Wednesday **hot brown**,
Tuesday sorghum,
Monday burgoo.

All you lucky children
come and eat it up.
Come and eat it up!

Today Is Thursday.

Today is Thursday.
Thursday **Bibb lettuce**,
Wednesday hot brown,
Tuesday sorghum,
Monday burgoo.

All you lucky children
come and eat it up.
Come and eat it up!

Today Is Friday.

Today is Friday.
Friday **rolled oysters**,
Thursday Bibb lettuce,
Wednesday hot brown,
Tuesday sorghum,
Monday burgoo.

All you lucky children
come and eat it up.
Come and eat it up!

Today Is Saturday.

Today is Saturday.
Saturday **Derby-Pie®**,
Friday rolled oysters,
Thursday Bibb lettuce,
Wednesday hot brown,
Tuesday sorghum,
Monday burgoo.

All you lucky children
come and eat it up.
Come and eat it up!

Today Is Sunday.

Today is Sunday.
Sunday **spoon bread**,
Saturday Derby-Pie®,
Friday rolled oysters,
Thursday Bibb lettuce,
Wednesday hot brown,
Tuesday sorghum,
Monday burgoo.

All you lucky children come and eat it up. Come and eat it up! Come and eat it up!

Word Menu

Bibb lettuce

Originally called Limestone lettuce for the soil in which it is grown, this small variety of butter-head lettuce was developed by John B. Bibb in his garden in Frankfort circa 1865. The most popular way of serving Bibb lettuce is "wilted" with fresh green onions in a warm bacon and vinegar dressing.

Burgoo

Burgoo is a thick, spicy meat and vegetable stew often slow cooked in large pots outdoors over an open flame for large social gatherings.

Derby-Pie®

A registered trademark dessert of Louisville's Kern's Kitchen, this rich chocolate and walnut pie was created by George Kern and his parents, Walter and Leaudra, as the specialty pastry of the Melrose Inn in Prospect, Kentucky. Since the 1950s, this treat has been traditionally served on Kentucky Derby Day, the first Saturday in May.

Hot brown

An open-faced sandwich with turkey, ham, bacon, pimentos, tomato, and a cheese sauce that is placed under the broiler, this dish was created by Chef Fred K. Schmidt at the Brown Hotel in Louisville to serve guests and musicians late at night after dinner dances.

Rolled oysters

First served at Mazzoni's Café, this "only in Kentucky" sandwich is made with three or four Chesapeake Bay oysters placed inside a cornmeal batter called "pastinga." The baseball-sized battered oysters are then rolled in a cracker-crumb coating and deep fried until brown and served with cocktail sauce.

Sorghum

A "must" on breakfast biscuits, this molasses is an eastern Kentucky Appalachian substitute for maple syrup.

Spoon bread

Made with cornmeal, eggs, and butter, this soft cornbread is a cross between pudding and bread. It is served piping hot from the oven with butter and is eaten with a spoon.

Other foods associated with Kentucky are Kentucky fried chicken, Benedictine sandwich, mutton barbeque, Ale-8-One, Shaker lemon pie, green tomato pie, stack cake, beaten biscuits, ham an' biscuits, jam cake, cheese garlic grits, cheeseburgers, and chocolate gravy.

Today Is Monday In Kentucky

Traditional song with adapted lyrics by Johnette Downing
© 2010 Johnette Downing, Wiggle Worm Records

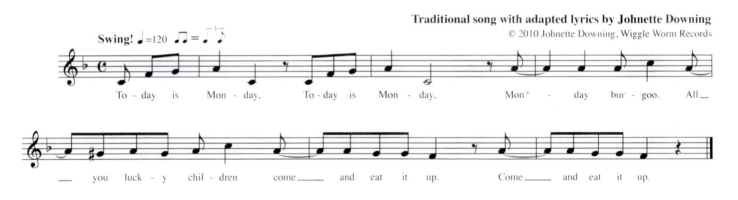

To-day is Mon-day, To-day is Mon-day, Mon-day bur-goo. All __ you luck-y chil-dren come __ and eat it up. Come __ and eat it up.